Uncle Jethro's Guide to the Sixth Sense

Awakening Your Intuition

Uncle Jethro's Guide to the Sixth Sense

Awakening Your Intuition

Jethro & Kay Smith

ReadersMagnet, LLC

Uncle Jethro's Guide to the Sixth Sense: Awakening Your Intuition
Copyright © 2019 by Jethro & Kay Smith

Published in the United States of America
ISBN Paperback: 978-1-950947-19-5
ISBN eBook: 978-1-950947-20-1

All rights reserved. No part of this publication may be reproduced, stored in a retrieval system or transmitted in any way by any means, electronic, mechanical, photocopy, recording or otherwise without the prior permission of the author except as provided by USA copyright law.

The opinions expressed by the author are not necessarily those of ReadersMagnet, LLC.

ReadersMagnet, LLC
10620 Treena Street, Suite 230 | San Diego, California, 92131 USA
1.619.354.2643 | www.readersmagnet.com

Book design copyright © 2019 by ReadersMagnet, LLC. All rights reserved.
Cover design by Ericka Walker
Interior design by Shemaryl Evans

DEDICATION

This book is dedicated to my beloved metaphysical teachers,
Meg, Abbey and Victor.

ACKNOWLEDGMENTS

Dora, Victor's mother, whose prayers and light work healed many.

Meg, whose wisdom and spiritual counseling gave
me the knowledge to walk in the Light.

Abbey, whose teaching abilities prepared me
for unexpected turns along the path.

Victor, whose strengths taught me discipline to do the right thing.
Always.

CONTENTS

1	About the Sixth Sense	1
2	How to Resonate at a Higher Frequency	4
3	Energy Centers of the Physical Body	9
4	Guide to Psychic Protection Protective Prayer	22
5	Guide to Using Dice as a Tool	24
6	Guide to Seeing Your True Colors–The Aura	33
7	Guide to Using Dominoes as a Tool	41
8	Guide to Using Playing Cards as a Tool	60
9	Guide to Reading the Palm as a Tool	95
10	Spiritual Cleansing	98

From The Author 103
About The Author 105

1

About the Sixth Sense

THE MYSTERY OF THE SIXTH SENSE

FACT OR FICTION, PARANORMAL OR INSTINCT, the sixth sense is a subject of the twenty-first century. Every person has at some point experienced an inner knowing, a gut feeling, a sense which cannot be explained. How far to develop or to suppress the sense is the controversial issue.

Scientifically, the mysteries of matter and energy are ever expanding, and with every scientific discovery even more of the unknown is revealed. But fear of the unknown, paradoxically, is considered by many to be the most ancient and the strongest emotion of mankind.

Ultimately, every individual must personally determine, whether based upon fear, faith, knowledge or a myriad of reasons, just how far to heed the inner voice and delve into the unknown realm and mystery of the sixth sense.

ABOUT UNCLE JETHRO

I was born with the ability to see, hear, and feel the energy and the colors of the aura surrounding people and inanimate objects. Logically, perhaps this stems from an overly developed pineal gland or from my family heritage of generations relying upon instinct and connected closely with nature. My mother, Blackfoot Native American Indian, and her grandmother planted, harvested and hunted, and they also instinctively knew where game could be found for dinner, quickly, and where and what the kids were up to at practically any moment.

I was also the recipient of unexplained metaphysical gifts which appeared after a near death experience. This not only heightened my ability to see metaphysical energies but also heightened the ability to hear, feel and communicate with energies that are politely labeled anomalies. Perhaps I, too, am an anomaly, but through personal experience it became clear to me that every person is born with the gift of the sixth sense, and this gift can be suppressed or developed to levels beyond the imagination.

Whether consciously or subconsciously, the sixth sense can be suppressed at an early age through upbringing and a variety of factors. Later in life, culture and belief systems also play a role, and for many people the perceived conflict with spirituality is without a doubt a major concern. It is a valid concern, because there are light energies and dark energies. Every day a person consciously makes decisions and choices, and every day a person must commit spiritually to walk in the light.

A decision to suppress metaphysical perceptions that are otherwise available through insight, however, is akin to closing one's eyes on a battlefield. Determining not to witness the reality of events taking place around you does not guarantee safe haven or comfort, at least long term. It is rarely a wise resolution for a healthy individual.

For those who do not believe in the afterlife or spiritual energies, consider that energy does not die, it simply changes from one form into another. A reservoir of water at an electrical power plant does not cease to exist, it simply changes from its H2O form into kinetic energy and into electricity. Mankind, too, is an energetic bundle of atoms and molecules resonating at a vibrational frequency. As your sixth sense develops, you will begin to see, hear, and feel energetic frequencies and extrasensory perceptions with clarity. You will see, hear, feel and sense metaphysical energies around you that bring such beauty and enrichment that it takes your breath away. You will see energies of negative intent sent through banal thoughts and emotions which stick like gum or splatter like acid when hitting the energy shield of an unsuspecting target.

Spiritual enlightenment is not closing your eyes, heart and mind to the reality of what is going on around you. Heightening your awareness and developing your sixth sense with positive, spiritual intent can enrich your faith, your life, and your ability and desire to help others and yourself.

2

How to Resonate at a Higher Frequency

THE FIRST STEP TOWARD HEIGHTENING YOUR sixth sense is to raise the vibrational frequency at which you resonate. Everything resonates at a vibrational frequency, and although these "vibes" are often sensed as a subtle feeling of "knowing," heightening one's own energetic vibration enables a person to see, hear and feel energetic frequencies and extrasensory perceptions with clarity.

If you could view the energy emanating from your physical body, called an aura, you would notice that the color of your energy fluctuates depending upon a variety of factors. Some factors are internal, and some factors are external.

INTERNAL FACTORS

Internal factors affecting your energy are those aspects emanating from within yourself, such as your emotional state of being. If you are feeling sad, your aura color will appear heavy and dark. Oftentimes, very dark blue hues of energy can change into your own aura color and back to the dark blues within a few moments. When you are "feeling the blues," you literally are feeling these shades of blues.

When you are feeling confused or defensive, your energies appear to be yellowish and will show a variety of other colors depending upon your situation. Let's say you are confused regarding a relationship. Your energy will appear to be yellow with a green heart energy because the subject that is confusing you is related to your heart, and the heart is a green energy center. Whereas if you are confused regarding your business decisions or career, your aura will appear to be yellow and orange because the subject which confuses you concerns your power, the sacral area at the base of your spine, which is an orange-colored energy center.

If you are feeling jealousy and insecurity toward another, your energies appear to absorb a greenish-yellow tinge.

Another internal factor affecting your vibrational energy is whether you are feeling physical pain. When a person is suffering from a severe headache, the colors surrounding the area of the neck and head often appear erratic. Instead of indigo and blue, which are the normal colors surrounding these two areas of the body, there will be flares of red and dark black bursts of energy. You can actually feel and hear the pulsing energies as the body fights the pain of the headache and the indigo energy tries to overcome the negative vibrational energy. In a severe migraine, the constant pulsating of the red energy pace can be so severe that the vibration is similar to the sounding of an alarm going off, both in rhythm and intensity.

Severe emotional pain can also affect the color of your energy. You will sometimes see a silver tinge around the indigo center if a person is grieving. I have personally come to the conclusion that those who are deeply suffering grief are actually feeling the energy of the upper chakras, the higher energy centers. This energy is so yearning to be out-of-body and with the person for whom they grieve that it is pulling the colors together, creating the silver tinge to their chakra.

Any of the heavy, negative energies can inhibit and block the flow of incoming perceptions to the senses and impede the sixth sense. The more clear the energy field surrounding the body, the more clear the perceptions of the sixth sense. It is much like viewing one's environment through a clouded, dark glass or through a crystal clear glass windshield.

EXTERNAL FACTORS

External impediments are also factors which can affect the flow of metaphysical impressions to the sixth sense. In effect, negative external energies can block the flow of incoming perceptions and lower a person's vibrational energy just as negative internal factors. Specifically, external negative intent but also external positive intent from other people directed toward you can affect both your aura field and the field surrounding your aura.

An example of external negative energy headed your way is when you walk into a room and the individuals who are already in the room have been arguing. That uncomfortable feeling of heavy energy is usually the color of red and orange. It is the orange power-energy intermixed with the red of anger. It can oftentimes make a person physically and mentally sick. Notice how a person living with someone who is mentally and physically abusive will experience numerous types of illnesses, both mental and physical, because of the negative energy that is in the house and with the person who is violent.

Different plants and many times animals will sense the negative vibration more quickly than a human being. Have you ever walked your dog and suddenly the dog is reactive to an area over which you are walking for the first time. If you were able to analyze and step into the past, the place over which the animal is reacting is the location where a person or persons have experienced unpleasant negativity. This could have been a fight or perhaps the location where someone had actually been hurt. The energy would have remained and resonated, and your animal has simply picked up the residue from the people who were there originally. The animal is upset and is behaving protectively toward you, thus acting peculiar when there appears to be no sign of danger.

Humans can also share, exchange, and send and receive positive energy from an animal. Notice someone else's animal a good ten minutes before the owner arrives. You will notice the animal becoming more lively and attentive toward the door and more positively responsive toward you. The animal is receiving the positive and emotional sensations from its owner, even before the owner has arrived. The pet is communicating to the owner that it is there and can hardly wait for him or her to enter. This is why you will also notice, although sadly, when a pet's owner has passed away sometimes the animal cannot come out of the grief. The pet, too, may unfortunately pass away due to the strong sensations of grief the animal is experiencing.

YOUR TRUE COLORS

The color of your aura ideally should appear clear, crisp and vibrant, no matter which color. Certain meditations and prayer can help clear the energy field so that the color of your energy will become as clear and as positive as that of your character and your life choices.

If you are a heartfelt and emotionally-connected person, for instance, your aura will reflect a very strong, green energy because the heart center is usually the strongest energy center of the body. The heart center of the body appears green, sometimes green and pink. There will be other factors in addition to your character that affect your aura, such as your daily activities and patterns. Your career, for example, will play a role. If you are a verbal, career-oriented person such as a business professional, lawyer, telephone operator or public speaker, your aura will appear more blue because of the communication aspects of your career, the area of the throat being a blue-colored energy; whereas if you are a counselor, psychiatrist, professor or student, your aura will appear more yellow because you are a knowledge seeker.

If your aura colors appear faded, dingy or dull, this indicates you may have emotional, physical, and oftentimes spiritual ailments. Regular holistic exercises, prayers and meditations can transform the color and intensity of your vibration immensely. I have witnessed negative energy completely disappear from a person's aura with the help of spiritual and holistic treatments and prayers. Oftentimes the simple exercises set forth in the following chapters will help strengthen, clear and balance the aura so that negative vibrations can be released and kept out of the energy field.

3

Energy Centers of the Physical Body

THE FIRST EXERCISE FOR RAISING AND maintaining a higher vibrational frequency involves a basic chakra visualization. A chakra is simply the Sanskrit name for an energy center inside the physical body, of which we will focus on seven. Each of the seven chakras, or energy centers, is a different color. A chakra energy is not the aura energy. The aura is an oval-shaped energy field radiating outward from the physical body.

When I look at a person physically, I see first their outer aura. For example, upon meeting my fiancé for the first time after backpacking, she was pleased to discover that initially I do not see if someone is wearing make-up nor do I see lines, wrinkles and imperfections of the physical body. If I decide to raise my energy vibration, I can peer into the physical body's energy, somewhat like squinting, and view the person's chakras. There is some controversy on the number of chakras, the colors, and the rotation of the energies, but for the purpose of these exercises I will describe what I see, and you can personally adjust your meditation to fit your personal ideals.

THE SEVEN CHAKRAS

The seven energy centers, or chakras, within the physical body, in brief, are:

> Seventh Chakra - Purple - Crown - Dreams, Astral
>
> Sixth Chakra - Indigo - Third Eye - Psychic Intuition
>
> Fifth Chakra - Blue - Throat - Communication
>
> Fourth Chakra - Green / Pink - Heart
>
> Third Chakra - Yellow - Solar Plexus - Intellect, Emotions
>
> Second Chakra - Orange - Sacral - Creative, Sexual, Power
>
> First Chakra - Red - Tail Bone - Basic Survival Issues, Grounding

If you are unfamiliar with holistic energy work of this type and have not yet experienced the ability to see or hear the energetic frequencies, the concept of chakra visualization could at first feel foreign and difficult to memorize.

Simply stated, if a frequency is vibrating fast enough, it is emitted as a color of light. If a frequency is vibrating slightly slower, it is emitted as a sound. The higher chakra energies, such as the seventh crown chakra, are resonating at a higher frequency than the lower chakra energies, such as the first root chakra.

Accordingly, each chakra vibration naturally resonates with and is associated with a different color, function and sound or musical note.

Holistic healers who have heightened their senses to see and hear energetic frequencies can testify to experiences with light and sound, where energy being removed from an individual can actually make physical sounds and react so as to appear to have a physical, material existence. While lecturing at a mind, body, spirit exposition on the topic of auras and resonating at a higher vibrational frequency, I noticed a person in the audience who had a very odd substance on her third eye. It was clear to me that she was not able to see auras because of it.

I had never seen this substance. It looked like sticky gum or perhaps putty had been placed on her third eye. Because I was standing very close to her and felt assured that the higher spiritual guides and angels would help me with this, I asked her permission to remove this substance. After she gave her permission I removed the sticky substance, and as I did so it emitted a sound like the slurping of a bathtub drain which had suddenly become unplugged.

I was further impressed at how quickly the woman was able to see auras. She immediately expressed that she was seeing my aura for the first time. As this was a very heart-felt moment, I knew that my aura was very green. I asked her what color she was seeing. She was correct about the color of my aura at that moment and was correct with another individual who was standing in front of her when she correctly answered that his aura was also green and that the person beside him was blue.

She had undoubtedly been blocked by this substance and confided to me afterward that she believed her mother's intention was the cause of this substance being placed there. All she knew was that her mother had never believed that an individual could see an aura, even though her grandmother had been able to see auras and had repeatedly declared how the two of them were alike. She felt that her mother was able with negative determination to project this substance upon her third eye, thus blocking her ability to see up until this point.

Another example was while working with a subject who had not been feeling well for some time. I saw and knew that it was because of a dark substance that seemed to be connected to her heart chakra in her upper back. The substance looked like a cocoon of a very dark, grayish nature. It was approximately fourteen to fifteen inches long and four to five inches wide. I did the same as I did with the person previously mentioned at the health exposition. I raised light energy, reached with her permission to this obstacle and surrounded the obstacle with white light, pulling the obstacle away from the individual to whom it was attached.

We were both surprised to hear a loud suction sound as if something similar to an extremely large suction cup that had been holding on to a slippery surface had suddenly released. The sound was very much audible, and this particular person had never experienced hearing a metaphysical frequency prior to this point in time. We both heard the same sound at the same time, and I realized that what I had pulled off of her was no longer attached. I could tell immediately from her aura that she was now no longer giving this substance energy but was actually back to just her energy within her own aura.

There are many circumstances of what I call psychic surgery where individuals have had substances, entities, links and even what appear to be other creatures attached to them which can be released and removed. Through the help of my spiritual guides and angels I have personally been able to help remove these objects unless the guides and angels inform me that it would harm the person to do so.

If there is ever any doubt of an unhealthy energy that is being felt or sensed, the simple rule is to pray and to send light. Not every person has developed or been given the gift of healing, but every person can pray and send light to another individual with the positive intention of helping and healing.

GUIDE TO CHAKRA VISUALIZATION

Eventually you will be able to feel, hear, and see the chakra energies and the colors surrounding you, which powerfully validates what you already sense from your gut feeling and intuition. The visualization exercise provided in this chapter is intended to greatly speed up this process for you.

There are three steps to the visualization exercise. Each step is repeated for each of the seven chakras before moving to the next chakra in sequence. The entire exercise is laid out fully at the end of this chapter. To first summarize, the three steps entail the basic creative ability to visualize in a safe, quiet place the following:

1. Visualize the chakra center in your body, imagining its location and color, spinning slightly in a clockwise direction.

2. Visualize inhaling pure light energy into the color of the chakra. Inhale slowly through your nose to the count of seven, imagining light energy purifying the color of the chakra. Pause, holding your breath for a brief moment.

3. Exhale slowly through your mouth to the count of seven. Visualize exhaling anything that is not light. Blow the energy out through your mouth as though you were blowing out birthday candles on a cake.

After the first chakra only, the red chakra, you will visualize grounding the new energy. Grounding is similar to the principle of cell memory when an athlete is learning a new sport or is unlearning improper form that has been developed. The correct technique is practiced repeatedly until muscle memory enables the athlete to automatically resort to the proper technique, thus no longer needing to consciously focus on each specific movement every time the action is performed.

Grounding is vital to retain the energy at the higher frequency. In time, you will no longer need to perform the chakra visualization before every metaphysical exercise, but it is especially important in the beginning. The chakra visualization is a necessary key, without which you will not develop the ability to see, hear, feel and most importantly, to read the energies of the metaphysical frequencies for any length of time, thus limiting your experience to mere moments of insight, the psychic flash, and quick, intuitive first impressions.

THE MIRROR TEST

Extra tip: It is vitally important to perform the meditation exercise. It is equivalent to the gas in your engine, the wind behind your sails. This is what enables you to enter into areas of your psychic abilities and work with your sixth sense to actually sense and feel your energies. For example, perform this simple exercise to experience how this energy works.

Go to your bathroom mirror and with no lighting behind you, look at the mirror without intensely staring at it. Relax, and not really focusing on anything in particular, gently move from one foot to the other, slowly moving your body in a very casual, rhythmic, relaxed state, looking at your outer aura, which is one or two inches outside of your body and your head. Look and notice what color you see.

If you have not begun the chakra exercises, you will very seldom see much of anything, but if you practice the meditations of the chakra exercise in this book for even just ten minutes, less than two minutes per chakra, you will be able to see the white energy of your outer aura and oftentimes the colors of your inner chakras. This alone is why you must not skip this exercise. You could miss the whole purpose of seeing your aura and using the chakra exercise to heighten your psychic abilities and sixth sense.

CHAKRA VISUALIZATION EXERCISE
FIRST CHAKRA

a. Focus on your first chakra. This chakra is located at the base of your tail bone and is red. This chakra rules basic survival issues and grounding energies. Visualize the red energy spiraling slightly in a clockwise direction.

b. Imagine inhaling pure light energy into the red chakra. Inhale slowly through your nose to the count of seven, imagining light energy purifying the red color of the chakra. Pause, holding your breath for a brief moment.

c. Exhale slowly through your mouth to the count of seven. Visualize exhaling anything that is not light.

d. Repeat this for a total of three times, pouring light energy into your red chakra.

e. Before moving to the next chakra, ground your energies. Grounding your energies enables you to maintain the heightening of your sensations. Visualize lines of red energy like the roots of a tree or a plant. Visualize these roots of light moving down through your legs and feet into the ground and down into the core of the earth. The stronger the visualization, the stronger your new vibrations will hold. After you have secured your grounding, begin to focus on your second chakra.

SECOND CHAKRA

a. Focus on your second chakra. This chakra is located two inches below your belly button and is orange. This is your sensual, sexual and power chakra. Visualize orange energy spiraling slightly in a clockwise direction.

b. Imagine inhaling pure light energy into the orange chakra. Inhale slowly through your nose to the count of seven, imagining light energy purifying the orange color of the chakra. Pause, holding your breath for a brief moment.

c. Exhale slowly through your mouth to the count of seven. Visualize exhaling anything that is not light.

d. Repeat this for a total of three times, pouring light energy into your orange chakra. After you have finished, move on to your third chakra.

THIRD CHAKRA

a. Focus on your third chakra. This chakra is located three inches above your belly button. It is yellow and rules your intellect and emotions. Most of your psychic impressions will come from here, especially concerning other people. Visualize yellow energy spiraling slightly in a clockwise direction.

b. Imagine inhaling pure light energy into the yellow chakra. Inhale slowly through your nose to the count of seven, imagining light energy purifying the yellow color of the chakra. Pause, holding your breath for a brief moment.

c. Exhale slowly through your mouth to the count of seven. Visualize exhaling anything that is not light.

d. Repeat this for a total of three times, pouring light energy into your yellow chakra. After you have finished, move on to your fourth chakra.

FOURTH CHAKRA

a. You are now at your fourth chakra, your heart chakra, located directly in the center of your chest. It is green with sometimes a bit of pink surrounding it. The heart chakra controls all of the energy that flows into your life and similar to your physical heart, it disburses energy throughout your body and into all of your other chakras. It is the basis for your spiritual beliefs and resonates most to the higher being. Visualize green energy and pink energy of unconditional love spiraling slightly in a clockwise direction.

b. Imagine inhaling pure light energy into the green and pink chakra. Inhale slowly through your nose to the count of seven, imagining light energy purifying the green and pink colors of the chakra. Pause, holding your breath for a brief moment.

c. Exhale slowly through your mouth to the count of seven. Visualize exhaling anything that is not light.

d. Repeat this for a total of three times, pouring light energy into your green and pink chakra. After you have finished, move on to your fifth chakra.

FIFTH CHAKRA

a. Now you are at the fifth chakra, which is located at your throat. This is a blue chakra and rules your communication. Visualize blue energy spiraling slightly in a clockwise direction.

b. Imagine inhaling pure light energy into the blue chakra. Inhale slowly through your nose to the count of seven, imagining light energy purifying the blue color of the chakra. Pause, holding your breath for a brief moment.

c. Exhale slowly through your mouth to the count of seven. Visualize exhaling anything that is not light.

d. Repeat this for a total of three times, pouring light energy into your blue chakra. After you have finished, move on to your sixth chakra.

SIXTH CHAKRA

a. You are now at your sixth chakra, which is located at the center of your forehead, a little off-center to the right. This chakra is the color of indigo and rules your psychic abilities. Visualize indigo energy spiraling slightly in a clockwise direction.

b. Imagine inhaling pure light energy into the indigo chakra. Inhale slowly through your nose to the count of seven, imagining light energy purifying the indigo color of the chakra. Pause, holding your breath for a brief moment.

c. Exhale slowly through your mouth to the count of seven. Visualize exhaling anything that is not light.

d. Repeat this for a total of three times, pouring light energy into your indigo chakra. After you have finished, move on to your seventh chakra.

SEVENTH CHAKRA

a. You are now at your seventh chakra that is three inches above your head. This is your crown chakra, and it is the color purple. It rules your dreams and astral abilities. Visualize purple energy spiraling slightly in a clockwise direction.

b. Imagine inhaling pure light energy into the purple chakra. Inhale slowly through your nose to the count of seven, imagining light energy purifying the purple color of the chakra. Pause, holding your breath for a brief moment.

c. Exhale slowly through your mouth to the count of seven. Visualize exhaling anything that is not light.

d. Repeat this for a total of three times, pouring light energy into your purple chakra.

After completing the entire exercise for each of the seven chakras, you are ready for the next step, which is psychic protection and prayer. I do, however, encourage you after the chakra visualization to also visualize a positive, strong armor sent to you from the higher being to protect you now that you have raised your light energies to a higher frequency.

SHIELDING

Once you have completed the visualization exercise of the chakras and the shield of armor, you should ideally refrain from activities where you must go out into the world. Avoid grocery stores, shopping malls and other public places. If you must go into a public domain, first take the extra measure of what is called psychic shielding.

Psychic shielding is essential because you will want to shield and focus yourself in a way that automatically protects your aura from others. Not everyone is a psychic vampire, which is a slang term for someone who pulls and taps your energy from you, but it is best to maintain a protection. Oftentimes people will attempt to take from your energy even unintentionally. This could be from a stranger who is having health problems, having a bad day or down on their luck and feeling depressed, and you are a very strong, light energy. Unfortunately the usual response is to pull energy from the stronger light energy. If you have been doing these exercises correctly, your energy will be very high and white.

When someone, whether a loved one or a stranger, is tapping your energy, you will usually feel depleted, worn out and unusually drained of your own energy. You will oftentimes be able to sense a link. When you are attempting to look at your energy as discussed in this guide book, you will notice that by looking at your hands, one hand will be lighter than the other. The hand that is not as light will be the side from which you are being tapped.

PSYCHIC SHIELD VISUALIZATION

Place your hands straight out in front of you at chest height. The distance between your hands should be the width of a basketball. Visualize in between your hands an energy that is strong and white, the same light energy you have been placing into your chakras.

If you have ever made a snowball, do the same now with the light energy. Push the energy from both of your hands into the white-light snowball that you are creating. Push the energy beginning from the size of a basketball, compressing it into the space of a regular-sized snowball that fits your hand.

Begin to see the energy change its color and texture, becoming a very strong, silver, reflective light mass. Begin to pull your hands apart from each other, slightly wider than your shoulders. Feel and sense this energy becoming a very intense ball in front of your head.

Pull your hands close to your body, close to your chest, and feel yourself becoming enveloped within this ball of energy. The energy expands to surround your entire body and aura. Depending upon how much energy you place into it, this can be a protective shield, a protective bubble that will protect you for many hours. As you become more adept at this exercise, it will protect your aura for days.

4

Guide to Psychic Protection Protective Prayer

As a young boy, I remember sitting in church with my godmother watching and enjoying the beautiful, clear energies vibrating from the pastor and from the people singing hymns. The color radiating from the preacher and the congregation was a light, sky blue that would turn into an electric blue, the electrifying blue color of a lightning storm, when the pastor began to speak passionately about what our Heavenly Father could do if the congregation only believed.

I have since seen this color of electric blue energy with many types of spiritual masters. I believe that for the Higher Creator to reach the masses, this energy is often used to stimulate clergymen, masters, and other spiritual orators in order to send out a message to the public of what the higher power wants the masses to hear.

These two steps, chakra meditation and protective prayer, should be performed before any metaphysical exercise. These measures ensure not only that you are grounded, focused and able to control the sensations as your metaphysical awareness heightens, but also that you are utilizing only the higher, positive, spiritual vibrations of the higher power. This further ensures that you are in a positive state and that you are being protected from negative influences that are active and could attempt to block, interfere, or steer your perceptions into a dark place. If you have done your grounding and protections, you will stay in the light.

Prayer is very personal and must be based upon your own conscience and your belief system. Traditionally, The Lord's Prayer is used by many. In addition to prayer, you may also visualize a protective shield around your entire body so as to keep the light in and the dark out. The protection you choose must include a higher light being such as a higher power, Christ's light energy, an archangel or a saint. You must request and ask a higher vibrational guardian consistent with your spiritual belief system in order for this to be successful.

Unlike the chakra meditation, which in time need not be performed before each and every exercise because you have successfully maintained a heightened energy frequency, the protective measure of prayer must always be done before reading energy and before every metaphysical encounter. Because of the constant flux of light and dark energies, the step of spiritual preparation is always performed before any exercise, never neglected.

If you are unsure of how to pray or meditate, find a quiet place and focus on receiving divine light and protection from the higher power. If you would like to recite prayer, a simple and effective prayer is The Lord's Prayer. Reciting this prayer with the proper intent will balance your energies and protect you from negativity regardless of your denomination.

The Lord's Prayer

Our Father, which art in heaven,
Hallowed be thy Name.
Thy Kingdom come.
Thy will be done in earth,
As it is in heaven.
Give us this day our daily bread.
And forgive us our trespasses,
As we forgive those that trespass against us.
And lead us not into temptation,
But deliver us from evil.
For thine is the kingdom,
The power, and the glory,
Forever and ever.

Amen.

5
Guide to Using Dice as a Tool

THERE ARE MANY TOOLS AVAILABLE TO help develop and safely practice using the sixth sense. A few of my favorite, basic tools are easy-to-find household items that will enable you to read an individual's energy and also to enjoy heightening your sixth sense while performing the exercises.

To clarify, all of the tools including the dice, the dominoes, and the playing cards are only objects that are being utilized by you and your own personal energy. The items are objects to use in order to help you focus your energies so that you are able to more fully utilize your abilities.

A tool is simply a neutral item to help assist with the task at hand. Employing the following tools will help you enjoy heightening your sixth sense so that you can use your abilities to help yourself and others.

REGULAR PLAYING DICE

In order to sense and project the future with regular dice, you will need five regular playing dice. The dice are easy to enjoy in that they are a fun, quick and positive way to look into your future.

This is the only tool where it does not matter whether the tool is new or whether it has been used previously by yourself or by others for entertainment. As we proceed to the other tools, such as the playing cards and dominoes, you will need to obtain the items new. If you do not already own an unused deck of playing cards or a set of unopened dominoes and would like to use these tools to practice reading energy, you will need to purchase a fifty-two playing card deck and a set of new dominoes.

In addition to the five dice and in addition to having completed your chakra meditation and protection prayer, you will need a flat, level surface upon which to roll the dice and to see which numbers the dice land upon.

To begin this exercise, hold the five dice in your dominant hand, the hand with which you use to write. Concentrate on the question you wish to ask. It could be any question such as, Will I get a new job, Will my relationship be successful, or Will I marry the person I have chosen. Concentrate on your question while holding the dice. It is good to charge and infuse the dice with your question and energy for at least three to four minutes.

After you have charged the dice and focused on your question, put the dice into your opposite hand, all five dice, and without looking directly at the dice, pick three dice out of the five in your hand. Concentrating on the question you wish to ask, roll those three dice.

You will learn to read the three dice in sequence from left to right. You will then create a sentence or phrase based upon the sequence, and the three dice together will tell the story. To do this, you will need to know the meaning of each die that is rolled and the meaning of the position of each die that is rolled.

INTERPRETING THE DICE

The meanings of the dice are as follows:

One signifies male, one is spiritual, definitely time to take action.

Two signifies female, relationship, yes to love.

Three signifies holy energy, healing energy, excellent health.

Four signifies housing, business, great news.

Five signifies power, strength, money.

Six signifies creativity, children, learning.

As the dice are rolled, your die should lay in order of left to right, position one, two, and three, respectively. Position one is the die furthest to your left, position two is the middle die, and position three is the die furthest to your right.

1. The far left position, position one, signifies the subject.

2. The middle position, position two, signifies how the subject relates to you.

3. The far right position, position three, signifies the outcome.

Put all three together, taking into consideration both the meaning of the dice and the position of the dice in the roll. Use your creativity and intuition. Also be aware while interpreting the dice that the definition provided may be symbolic rather than literal.

Any time you roll all three dice together and all three dice are the same number, the meanings are as follows:

Three ones indicate you are on a spiritual path, and the guides and angels are with you at all times. Yes to your question.

Three twos together indicate you are in a relationship that is true love. Hang on to this relationship at all costs.

Rolling all threes together indicates your health will improve and you will begin to feel more alive than you ever have.

Rolling four all together indicates business can be very good, but watch your assets. Someone is trying to handle your business.

Three fives together indicate power of the force is with you, but you will hear bad news. Not a good roll of dice.

Three sixes together indicate new beginnings in your life. You will begin learning many new ways to handle situations. Take special heed to your instinct at this time. Six can go either way. This could be a good opportunity for you or this could be a karmic lesson. Only time will tell.

THE POSITION OF THE DICE IN THE ROLL

Each number of dots has a different meaning based upon the position of the dice in the roll.

Number one of the dice:
Left position signifies the higher power;
Middle position signifies male;
Right position signifies boss or owner.

Number two of the dice:
Left position signifies relationship, spiritual love;
Middle position signifies female;
Right position signifies relationship.

Number three of the dice:
Left position signifies higher guidance;
Middle position signifies health;
Right position signifies karmic lesson.

Number four of the dice:
Left position signifies house, building, structure;
Middle position signifies business structure;
Right position signifies take heed and obey the rules.

Number five of the dice:
Left position signifies power;
Middle position signifies a business decision;
Right position signifies bad news concerning your work; new job situation on the horizon.

Number six of the dice:
Left position signifies creativity;
Middle position signifies child;
Right position signifies hard times coming, you will learn a great deal from this situation.

The dice can be rolled as many times as you feel it is necessary to continue asking questions in order to know your future. But a word of caution. Only ask the same question a maximum of three times, and accept the answer of two out of three for your question. Rolling the dice more than that will leave you with a confusing outcome.

As you interpret the dice, take into consideration the meaning of the die plus the meaning of the position of that die on the roll. For example, you rolled a four, furthest left position. Four signifies housing, business, great news. The die closest to your left is the first position. A four die in the first position means that the subject is a house or a building.

Use common sense and intuition as you combine the connotation of all three dice. Keep in mind that the far left position is the subject; the middle position is how the subject relates to you; and the third, right position is the outcome. Put all three together to construct a sentence or phrase.

Consider, as an example, that your first roll of three dice is 4 4 1.

A four in the first position means that the subject is regarding a structure, a house or a building. A four in the second position means it relates to you in the area of business, perhaps your career. And a number one die in the third position signifies a boss or an owner. The number one also signifies a male.

You would interpret this as someone in the business where you work is male and has something to do with your future concerning business; something about the place of business where you work, a male.

Take it deeper into the second roll to be more specific in your question regarding the first roll. Now you might ask, What does the man at my business have in store for me? What is his intention for me?

UNCLE JETHRO'S GUIDE TO THE SIXTH SENSE: AWAKENING YOUR INTUITION

You will need to repeat the exercise, this time asking, What does this man in my business have to do with me? If you are not rolling any dice that relate in any shape or form to your question, you have not fully charged and infused your energy and questions into the dice. Re-infuse the dice in your hand.

Go deeper with the next roll of the dice such as, How will this man affect my business? What is his intention for me? You will roll a second time, and then you have only one more roll so that you do not confuse the reading.

On the second roll, you ask, What is this man in my business intending to do? In your second roll, the sequence is 2 1 6.

Die number two in the first position means the subject is a relationship. Die number one in the second position signifies a man. This is regarding your relationship with a man. The last die being a six, the man who is in a relationship with you is in a career field that has to do with creativity or inventions, with a negative outcome for you.

You now know where or who this man is. If you are still unclear, you may roll one last time for your three-time roll of dice. At this time, ask for more clarity about the man who is affecting your business.

Third roll of three dice, this time you roll three fives. As you have seen, three fives is not good. This man is trying to get you fired in your business. You need to watch carefully because obviously you are being warned to take heed that some male in your business is out to get you. If you still have no idea who this man is, wait twenty-four hours and roll the dice again. Or better yet, practice with one of the other tools in this guide book with respect to the same subject.

You most often will find your own answers within the different types of tools. If all of that fails, my advice is to find outside counsel, someone whom you know and trust, to help you take correct and positive measures to ensure your successful future.

6

Guide to Seeing Your True Colors—The Aura

THE ABILITY TO SEE AURAS AND energy is an excellent tool and reduces the need to try to interpret sensations and feelings. It is easy to determine if the energy is a negative vibration coming your way or coming toward a loved one when you actually can see what looks like tobacco spit or a dark mass hit one's energy shield. Likewise, it is tremendously heartwarming to witness a healing energy and to witness spiritual love transforming the energetic vibrations of a loved one.

SEEING WITHOUT LOOKING

For this exercise, you will need a candle, any size and shape will do, as long as the candle has no candle holder. A tapered candle or a votive without the decorative holder will work just fine.

When selecting your candle, I suggest that you choose a white candle. White contains all colors of the visible spectrum and reflects light. Black is the opposite and absorbs light. Considering the purpose of the candle for this exercise, a white candle is preferred so that you will be able to most easily see your aura.

You will also need a quiet space where you can sit in a relaxed state, preferably in your home, although it is not necessary for you to perform this exercise at home. This exercise requires only that you are in a comfortable, quiet, safe space.

You will need: a candle; a lighter; a comfortable space.

As with all of these exercises, first complete the basic chakra meditation provided in this guide book. The basic chakra enhancing meditation is the fuel for all of your metaphysical exercises. You are performing these exercises to raise your spiritual vibration which in turn enables you to heighten your sixth sense to read metaphysical energies.

The second step you will need to complete before attempting this exercise is to have prayed or to have recited a spiritual psychic protection prayer. From now on, when I refer to your chakra meditation and your protection prayer before attempting the exercise, you will know to have completed the basic chakra enhancing meditation and your choice of which protection prayer you will use.

Assuming that you have completed your chakra meditation and your protection prayer, you are ready to begin, now sitting comfortably in your room or quiet space. Please ensure that you have prepared the proper environment.

To optimize the effect of this exercise to see your own aura, place your feet at the same width as your shoulders. Sitting in a comfortable chair with your back relaxed in a comfortable position, lay your hands openly in front of you, as though you were waiting to receive a gift in your hands, which you will soon receive from your spiritual guides and angels.

With this exercise, you will begin to practice opening and utilizing your sixth chakra. The sixth chakra is known as your third eye, which enables you to see your own aura emanating from your body. Later, if you so choose, you will be able to practice seeing the auras of other individuals as well.

In the relaxed meditative state, feel your hands on your lap. With the candle lit before you, look at the candle flame. Do not look directly into the flame but look more at the outer edge of the flame.

Breathing-in light and positive energy through your nose, feel that energy filling your lungs, relax, still looking at the outer edge of the candle flame, and raise your hands up directly in front of you with your fingers wide spread as though you were catching a basketball. Then put your fingers closely together within an inch of touching, almost touching but not touching. Look down at your fingers and notice the energy in between your fingers. There between your fingers you will see the color of your aura.

This is the color of your aura at the very moment you are performing this exercise. Because there is always more than one emotion and spiritual sensation affecting our physical bodies and auras at any given time, you will need to repeat this exercise five to seven times. As you repeat this exercise, make a mental note of your aura and colors. This will be your personal aura pulse and sensation. You will be able to as I call it, dial-in to your personal aura and spiritual guides and angels once you know the color and pattern of your aura.

The color codes and descriptions are provided at the end of this chapter to enable you to decipher your color code pattern. Once you have completed the exercise five times and you were able to see some or all of the colors red, orange, yellow, green, blue, violet and purple, you will be able to refer to the color code descriptions to decipher aspects of your future or the person's future of whose aura you are reading. In addition, it is necessary to consider the positive and negative aspects of the colors you see in the energy around your fingers.

POSITIVE AND NEGATIVE ASPECTS OF COLOR

In order to read the colors of the aura, it is necessary to decipher the positive and the negative aspects of the chakra color. After you have completed your seeing-without-looking exercise five to seven times with the candle and have a definite color in mind, place your hands together.

Visualize the color as you saw it, and feel or sense what your solar plexus tells you about what you are feeling. Rely on your gut feeling about this color. A good practice is for you to place your hands in front of you again and visualize the color that you are experiencing. Allow yourself to simply relax, feel, and sense.

If you feel a cold or an odd sensation, that is a negative aspect of the color. If you feel nothing at all or if you feel positive, good sensations, that is the positive aspect of this color. In the world in which we live, there is a positive and negative aspect in everything.

Use this tool to help enhance you and tune you as an instrument to be better able to help yourself and to help others when sensing an individual's aura.

GUIDE TO DECIPHERING THE COLORS OF ENERGY

THE COLOR RED

When you see your aura exuding a red energy, this indicates you will need extra energy for the path ahead of you. Usually within seven days you will need to exert energy in your life for the next cycle. Particularly when the red energy is close to the left side of your body, which is the direction of incoming energy as compared to the right side of the body which is the direction of outgoing energy, you will need to exert extra energy for what is coming into your path. Oftentimes when the red is on the left side, you are seeing an indication of an event that is energy packed, a change such as a break-up in a relationship or a new job situation.

If you attempted the exercise of positive and negative and the focus was your red chakra, which is the root chakra located at your tail bone, and you experienced negative or odd, cold sensations, this indicates you are feeling threatened. You likely are in a survival mode. Alternatively, you are too controlling in your physical space and should practice working on grounding and letting go of physical limitations in your life and daily affairs.

THE COLOR ORANGE

Orange positive aspects: when you see orange, your creativity is at a high flow. This is a time to utilize your artistic and creative abilities. This is when you are more than ordinarily in a good creative space. Also connotes that you are sexually aroused or feeling powerful.

If you experience sensations with the orange color during the exercise and it is not a comfortable feeling but a cold or distant feeling, you are sexually inhibited. Alternatively, you are not currently able to express your creative desires. You should engage in some mental exercises such as drawing, creating, or expressing yourself in a way that enables you to feel good about yourself.

THE COLOR YELLOW

When seeing yellow and experiencing the positive aspects in your aura, you are mentally and intellectually high in energy and capable of taking-in a great amount of energy. You are very much a positive beacon and emotionally in-tune with your angels. Listen to your gut feeling at this time.

If you are not experiencing positive sensations with your yellow, this indicates that you are not in a good mental space right now. You should utilize music and art and other forms of mental stimulants to enable you to gain a more positive mental outlook. Remember never to mix alcohol or drugs of any form while endeavoring this exercise. Only stimulate with natural, positive events.

THE COLOR GREEN

Green energy surrounding your fingers signifies that you are very much in your space of higher being. You are working at healing yourself and the other chakra energies are being utilized also to heal yourself. You are in your sacred space. This is where all of your psychic readings should be done, from your heart chakra, because you are in more of a sacred space and not in an emotional or mental state, thus clouding the reading for someone else.

When you are reading for someone from your heart chakra, what you are saying and feeling may make no sense to you mentally or emotionally. It does, however, make sense to the person whose energy you are reading and that person is feeling and sensing exactly what is intended. You will be correct every time you are reading from your heart.

If you are being guided from your intellect and mentally sense and express what you feel intellectually is proper, then you may not be correct because your path is so different than that of whom you are reading. It is incorrect because that which you are perceiving for them is that which you emotionally do not care for in your own life. You could be relaying your own emotional inclinations onto that person, even when that person does not share in your emotional or mental dislikes.

When seeing the color green and experiencing negative sensations of green, then you are not doing what your heart tells you. You are not following your heart. You should feel and know that love is there for you and find your higher power. Love thyself to love others, is the lesson with this chakra if you are not receiving positive sensations from the color green or the color pink.

THE COLOR PINK

When you see pink around your fingers and conclude that pink is the color of your aura, do not confuse this color with violet or purple. You must practice this exercise quite a bit to know that you are correctly seeing pink.

Perform the exercise again, and while re-visualizing the color you saw around your fingertips, use your solar plexus chakra to sense what you feel from that color. If the emotion you get back from it is very much a calming, positive emotion of love, you are seeing and experiencing pink. If you sense strong psychic vibrations, you are sensing violet, and if you feel excited when you emotionally sense this color, you also are experiencing violet. Pink is a very passive, calm feeling, while violet is a very action-oriented feeling.

THE COLOR BLUE

Continuing along for the next positive attribute is the color blue. If you are sensing the color blue as your aura, you are a very communicative and positive individual. You are able to articulate what you need to express orally.

Using your solar plexus once again for this exercise, if you experience odd or cold, negative sensations from the color blue, you are shy or timid. Alternatively, you are not communicating what you need to say and should speak up in your life more at this time.

THE COLOR INDIGO

When experiencing the sensation and color of indigo, notice that it is sometimes difficult to distinguish between indigo and blue. A good rule of thumb is if you are seeing light blue such as sky blue, then you are seeing the color blue. If you are seeing very dark blue such as the color of a new pair of jeans, then you are seeing indigo.

The positive aspect of indigo is that you are seeing this color because you are very much open in your third eye. You have many psychic abilities that are just waiting for you to tap into.

If you felt odd, negative sensations when you saw indigo, you are in need of working with light workers and light warriors with regard to becoming friends with your spirit guides, angels and totem animals so that you can access and utilize all of your psychic abilities in a positive manner.

THE COLOR PURPLE

If you saw and experienced purple energies, you excel at the ability to remember your dreams. You are able to astral project, to go out-of-body and spiritually visit places so that you can help others with their life path.

If you experienced negative sensations while performing the exercise and seeing purple, you have difficulties with your dreams. Your guides and angels would like for you to clear your energy field. Seek and find a strong professional light worker to help you balance and cleanse your chakras. Your purple chakra is being "capped" from above and is not receiving all of the light vibrations that you as a light creature have the right and power to receive from your higher power.

THE COLOR VIOLET

If you saw violet energy, you are very much working with the higher powers of chemistry in that the angels and higher beings are around you and working with you in your daily affairs.

If you experienced a negative sensation from the violet aura color, you need to meditate and communicate more to the angels and guides to be better able to understand your mission in life.

THE COLOR OF LIGHT

Seeing light and positive colors in a positive way indicates you are very much wired-in and loved by the angels and guides above.

If you experienced negative or odd sensations when seeing the light colors, you did not perform a strong enough protection meditation. You need to work with the Higher Creator, Christ energy, or a strong archangel such as the Archangel Michael or if you prefer, work with eagle totem magic or Quan Yin or Master Buddha. You should seek out prayers and mantras that help you strengthen your connection with the light.

7

Guide to Using Dominoes as a Tool

A SET OF DOMINOES CONTAINS TWENTY-EIGHT dominoes. For this metaphysical exercise, you will need a special bag in which to store the set of dominoes. Any storage bag or even a brown paper bag will suffice. You will need to purchase a new set of dominoes containing twenty-eight dominoes.

It is important not to use a set of dominoes which has been used for playing. You want to infuse the dominoes with your energy and intent so that the dominoes will only be used as a tool to see your own future and that of others. If you have used the dominoes to play a game of dominoes for entertainment, the dominoes have already been infused with the energy of all of the people who have played with them and are now a tool to be used for amusement only.

As in the previous exercises, first complete the chakra visualization and then your protection prayer. This is followed with a five to ten minute positive meditation where you sit with your domino set, an unopened, newly purchased package, and hold your packaged set in both hands. Infuse the dominoes with your light intent and positive vibration. Focus on the idea and intent of using the dominoes as a tool to see and to foretell the future for yourself and for others.

A positive, fundamental aspect of using the dominoes as a tool is, like the dice, you may ask the question and then go deeper with the following question to find your answers. But also like the dice, only ask the same question or the question pertaining to the original question a maximum of three times so as not to cloud or confuse your psychic forecast.

To begin the exercise, and after you have infused your new set of dominoes with your energy, open the package and put each domino one by one into the special bag. As you pull out each domino individually, each domino will be infused by your touch with your energy and intention as you place it into the sack. Concentrate on infusing each domino with your energy as you touch it and place it into the sack.

You may put the dominoes into any kind of sack, even a brown paper bag from the grocery store, or if you have a pillowcase that has not been used, use the pillowcase as a means to hold and store your new dominoes. Be sure, once again, to use a new pillow case, not one which you or someone else has slept upon because the pillowcase will need to be clear from all energies so as to store your new psychic tool. Placing the twenty-eight dominoes into the special sack should be a very positive experience.

Picking up each individual domino and feeling its positive energy, you will begin to sense the vibration of the domino. Remember to hold on to positive thoughts while doing this exercise. The more you put into this positive fusion, the more you will be able to accurately work with the dominoes. You will amaze yourself and others with how correct your future readings will be as you learn to enjoy this tool.

After you have placed all twenty-eight dominoes into the bag, move your hand into the bag and shake the bag, moving the dominoes, stirring them, feeling the energies within them. So as to enjoy this experience, you will need to be careful if you are using a brown paper bag from the store. It will not wear well if you are very physical as you stir the dominoes, and it will tear. After you have turned the dominoes a couple of times with your hand and tumbled them around in the sack, lay the domino bag down.

With your dominant hand reach into the domino bag, pulling out three dominoes one at a time, placing the first domino on the left, the second domino to its right, and the third domino to the far right. Three dominoes, being aware of which domino is first, second and third.

As you lay the three dominoes in front of you from left to right, the first domino is furthest to your left and is in position one. The second domino is in the middle, position two, and the third domino is your furthest right domino, position three.

> The far left position represents the subject matter.
>
> The middle position represents how the subject relates to you.
>
> The third, right position represents the outcome.

Each domino is divided in half with a number of dots from zero to six on each half of the domino. Each pair of numbers has a significance, which is set forth at the end of this chapter. As you read and interpret the layout of the dominoes, keep in mind the meaning of the left, middle and right positions as well as the meaning of each number and each pair of numbers on the respective domino.

SYMBOLIC SIGNIFICANCE OF THE NUMBERS

Also be aware while interpreting the dominoes that the definition provided may be symbolic rather than literal. For example:

0. Dots is not a favorable domino. Oftentimes the outcome of the question you are asking is not what your guides feel you should be focusing on at this time.

1. Dot is your higher power and sense of spiritually but can also mean a male, oftentimes a person who is connected with you in a strong way.

2. Dots is involving a relationship. It usually signifies a female but also can signify a man who is very sensitive.

3. Dots involves your spirituality but it could also refer to your physical health.

4. Dots could represent your personal home where you reside, or it could represent something material with four corners such as a dwelling or a business.

5. Dots is your own ability to handle the situation and the power to get through anything and to receive any and all things that you want. But the numeral five has to do with power and timing. Depending upon where it falls with the other dominoes, you will get through the situation but you may or may not get all that you want.

6. Dots represents a child, but it could also represent a youthful or an immature person or a childlike person or someone who is not acting his or her age.

LITERAL SIGNIFICANCE OF THE NUMBERS

Keeping in mind that the significance of the number of dots represented on the dominoes may be symbolic rather than literal, the general significance of the numbers is as follows:

0. Blank means it is out of your hands. Because the future event is out of your hands, you have no control over what is going to happen.

1. Number one means male, one is spiritual, definitely time to take action.

2. Number two means female, relationship, yes to love.

3. Number three means holy energy, healing energy, health.

4. Number four means housing, business, great news.

5. Number five means power, strength, money.

6. Number six means creativity, children, learning.

As you look at the dominoes, notice if there are any patterns. For this exercise, we will use a very fundamental way of reading the dominoes.

You can also choose, however, to read a simplified version of the blank dominoes. If you draw a blank in the first position, as in both sides of the domino are blank, then you have received your answer as no. If you draw a blank and it is in the middle position, then the answer is maybe. You will have your question answered soon. If you draw a blank and it is in the third position, you will need to consider asking the question at a later time.

When using the dominoes as a tool, remember that you can continually use the dominoes to ask further questions, but please do not continually keep asking the same question. Ask the same question only three times in a twenty-four hour period and then leave your question for another day. Accept the two-out-of-three domino forecast as your answer to what will happen.

Do not let anyone else use these dominoes. These dominoes are for you only to use to read your future and the future of others. Keep them in a safe place covered within the domino bag and away from outside energies so as to be used as an effective tool to heighten your intuitive abilities. Enjoy the dominoes.

THE POSITION OF THE DOMINOES

0-0

1. First position signifies this is not a good time for you to ask about this subject. Ask the question differently or ask something else.

2. Second position signifies the subject matter will not matter as much to you later as it appears to matter to you now.

3. Third position signifies the question you have asked is out of your hands. The question you have asked is not answerable right now, and the final outcome is out of your hands.

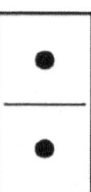

1-1

1. First position signifies a personal spiritual question, unity with a higher power.

2. Second position signifies how this relates to you with your basic spiritual needs. Yes, this is good for your spiritual needs.

3. Third position signifies you will have an awakening with your higher power over this. This is the outcome.

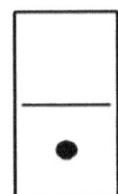
1-0

1. First position signifies a male who is not on your side.

2. Second position signifies a male who will go against you.

3. Third position signifies you will make an enemy of a male.

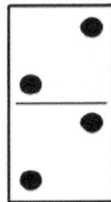
2-2

1. First position signifies very much a female working in your favor.

2. Second position signifies this is working with your feminine side. This is good for you.

3. Third position signifies the female involved with you will be on your side the whole way.

2-1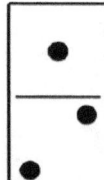

1. First position signifies your question involves a strong female.

2. Second position signifies a female who is spiritual is on your side, this is how it relates to you.

3. Third position signifies a female will be involved helping you in the outcome.

2-0

1. First position signifies a female who is not on your side.

2. Second position signifies a female who will cause problems regarding your question.

3. Third position signifies a female involved in this outcome will be your enemy. The outcome of this is that you will make an enemy of a female about whatever you asked.

3-3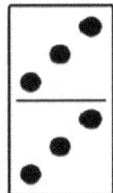

1. First position signifies a spiritual healing is coming your way.

2. Second position signifies it relates to you; you will become closer to your higher power than you have ever known.

3. Third position signifies the outcome; the Holy Spirit is on your side and favoring what you are asking.

3-2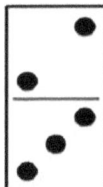

1. First position signifies be aware of your sensitive side when asking this question.

2. Second position signifies how it relates to you—your higher power is working to help you have a better relationship.

3. Third position signifies outcome—you will experience the benefits of a healthy, positive female helping you in this situation.

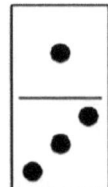

3-1

1. First position signifies there is a positive male spiritually helping you in this situation.

2. Second position signifies the question you are asking will help you become more connected to your higher power.

3. Third position signifies the outcome of this is that the Holy Spirit is working in your favor.

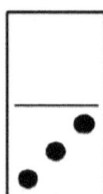

3-0

1. First position signifies the Holy Trinity is not in favor regarding the question you have asked.

2. Second position signifies you are becoming stronger than you ever knew. You will be much stronger when the outcome is completed.

3. Third position signifies you are working toward karma that has to be handled and this must be taken care of before you can move on.

4-4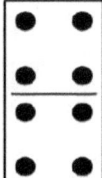

1. First position signifies you will be dealing with a very positive financial gain at home.

2. Second position signifies this relates to you in that you have an opportunity for advancement or positive job placement.

3. Third position signifies the outcome of your finances will become much better in the near future.

4-3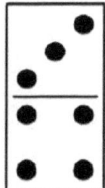

1. First position signifies your home life is going to be very much affected in a positive way over the question you have asked.

2. Second position signifies you will experience a newly found feeling of achievement when this has happened.

3. Third position signifies the outcome of your question will be very favorable for you.

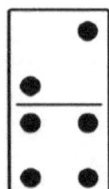

4-2

1. First position signifies a female in your house is not telling you everything.

2. Second position signifies a disappointment from a female very close to you in your home / family.

3. Third position signifies that as an outcome for your question, you will be put in a situation with a female that is not favorable for you.

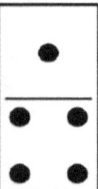

4-1

1. First position signifies a male in your house is not telling you everything.

2. Second position signifies a male in your house is not favorable toward what you asked in this question.

3. Third position signifies a male in your house will put you in a bad position over the question you have asked.

4-0

1. First position signifies your house and physical residence will change. You need to ask more from the dominoes.

2. Second position signifies this relates to your home and there will be a change in your household very soon.

3. Third position signifies the outcome of the question you asked will affect your house in a positive way. You need to pick three more dominoes and ask a stronger question regarding this subject.

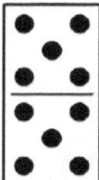

5-5

1. First position signifies you have the power in your hands to do anything you want right now. A very positive domino.

2. Second position signifies you are going to get whatever you have asked to happen, by your own means.

3. Third position signifies outcome, you have always had the ability to get what you have asked for. Yes, you will get it.

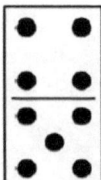

5-4

1. First position signifies there are powers working at your home that are in your favor.

2. Second position signifies the question you asked will be affecting your home situation in a good way.

3. Third position signifies you need to ask the dominoes a stronger question about your house. Yes, your house will have a positive change.

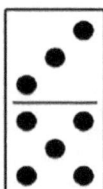

5-3

1. First position signifies the power of healing is working in your favor.

2. Second position signifies you will have a significant positive, healing experience.

3. Third position signifies your abilities to heal are being awakened. Continue with what you are doing now.

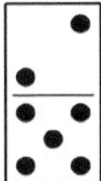

5-2

1. First position signifies a powerful woman is on your side.

2. Second position signifies you are going to have a positive woman of strength aiding you in this outcome of what you have asked.

3. Third position signifies yes, you will have the power of a relationship that will be unrivaled and make people jealous.

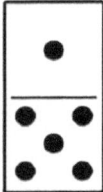

5-1

1. First position signifies that your outcome is positive and that a male is involved.

2. Second position signifies things are being handled by the higher power. Your fate is still undecided.

3. Third position signifies things out of your control and not in your favor. The answer is no.

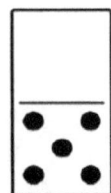

5-0

1. First position signifies the power is not in your favor. Do not attempt what you are asking. Do not do it.

2. Second position signifies the forces above do not feel it is the time for you to get what you are asking.

3. Third position signifies ask another question. This is not what you should have happen in your life at this time. Pull three more dominoes and ask a stronger question than you asked before.

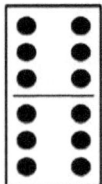

6-6

1. First position signifies children will be involved with what it is you are asking.

2. Second position signifies a child has the answer to what you seek.

3. Third position signifies children are involved and creativity is in your favor. Pick three more dominoes and ask a deeper question to what you have just asked. Creativity is in your favor right now.

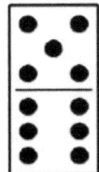

6-5

1. First position signifies you have the power of creativity on your side right now. Do continue with what you are asking.

2. Second position signifies you will creatively get a yes and work out what it is that you want to happen right now.

3. Third position signifies none are against you, and you can have it all if you want.

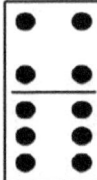

6-4

1. First position signifies someone younger in your house will come to your aid.

2. Second position signifies a child is involved. Be sure that you are listening to everyone's side of the story.

3. Third position, pull three more dominoes. Not everyone is being mature with what is happening.

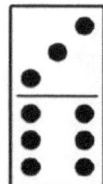

6-3

1. First position signifies a child's health is involved in what will happen with what you are asking.

2. Second position signifies someone is being immature but they will become more in your favor. It will soon turn in your favor.

3. Third position signifies the health of someone young will improve. You are helping to improve the health of someone who is younger.

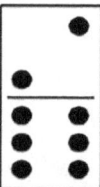

6-2

1. First position signifies a creative woman is involved in your question.

2. Second position signifies a woman will help you creatively with the outcome of this.

3. Third position signifies a woman will help you better understand yourself with this outcome.

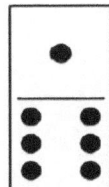

6-1

1. First position signifies a male child is involved with the outcome of this.

2. Second position signifies working with a male would be your best asset.

3. Third position signifies a younger male is involved in the outcome of this decision.

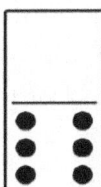

6-0

1. First position signifies this is not favorable for people who are your dependents. Do not do what you have asked in your question.

2. Second position signifies the outcome will not favor well with people who look up to you. You could be made a fool of if you continue to do what you have intended.

3. Third position signifies not a happy ending, but unfortunately you needed to go through this lesson in life. Pull three more dominoes to find out what else will happen from what you have done.

8
Guide to Using Playing Cards as a Tool

I LEARNED TO READ THE CARDS by working with my second metaphysical teacher, Abbey, who began working with me at the age of eight. I learned to use the fifty-two regular playing card deck for intuitive readings because I was unable to use the tarot deck. For some strange reason the energy from the tarot would not resonate with me, and I would feel physically ill after using them.

Please use my system, and enjoy yourself and the opportunity to use the playing cards to discover your own future events. Unlike the tarot, where it is advised against using the tarot to read your own fortune, the regular playing cards are an enjoyable tool and can be used for yourself as well as for others.

REGULAR PLAYING CARDS

Before reviewing the description of the playing cards, make sure that you are ready to begin this exercise. First, you must purchase a brand new deck of cards, a deck that has not been used by anyone for playing card games such as poker or solitaire. If the cards have been played with for games, then they have absorbed the energy from the person playing with them and are no good for fortune telling. That person's energy has been infused onto the cards, as well as the energy of the entire card game. Suppose, for example, the person wanted to draw four aces or the person intensely desired that a particular card show up in the pile. This intensity and intention of the card game would have contaminated the deck for the purpose of fortune telling.

For the fortune card reading you will need one deck of new playing cards. Immediately throw away all of the jokers and any blank cards that are in the deck. Also, it is advised to throw away the box in which the cards were packaged when you purchased them. Remember, you are changing these playing cards into a fortune telling tool. The cards will have a very positive and vibrant energy from you that you will be projecting onto the cards each time you use them as a metaphysical tool to show your future. You do not want to limit the tool to a box, because your fortune can be limitless if you choose.

You will also need a scarf or kerchief that has only been worn by you. If you really desire to energetically charge the cards with your family, you may use a scarf or kerchief of someone in your family who loved you very much who has passed on to the other side. But remember, that individual will be holding your fortune, so the possession of the deceased's scarf or kerchief should be from someone who loved you very much.

When I first tried this experiment, I was about nine or ten years old and chose a scarf from my deceased grandmother. When I was instructed that the person must love me very much, I was not sure how much she loved me, but I felt that she probably did. Long story short, I later discovered that my grandmother did not feel very partial toward me at all, and my card spreads were always very critical and very much upsetting to me.

Years later, I further discovered to my chagrin that the scarf had not even belonged to my grandmother but to her daughter. It was actually my aunt's scarf. This aunt was particularly critical toward me and had even given me the impression that she enjoyed upsetting me and making me cry. So, learn from my teacher and take my advice: if there is any question of who owns the scarf or any emotional feelings around it, please simply buy another scarf in your favorite color. Remember that you are looking into your own future, and you want it to be as positive and bright as your imagination can take you.

After you have thrown away the jokers and the blank cards, take the fifty-two cards and begin to know your cards. Do this by what is called the lazy man's shuffle or the overhand shuffle. This is simply a series of cutting the cards section by section in your hands until the cards are randomly shuffled. Never shuffle the cards as a dealer shuffles the cards, which scatters the energy. The overhand shuffle folds the energy into the cards.

While you are concentrating and mentally focusing on the question that you will ask, you should be doing the overhand shuffle and feeling the cards as a part of your energy.

After you have focused and shuffled for a good ten or fifteen minutes and your scarf is prepared, which is where you will wrap and store your cards once you have completed the exercise, you are ready to begin. I will provide three types of card readings.

PLAYING CARDS
THE YES AND NO CARD READING

The first card reading is the easiest and quickest for yes or no questions. This type of reading is very simple. Think of a yes or no question, and then concentrate on your question.

Cut the cards into three piles, placing the cards face down.

Next, turn only the top card face up on each of the three stacks. The color of the cards will determine if the answer is yes or no.

Perform this three times. Two out of three is confirmation of your yes or no answer. Do not perform this more than three times per question in a twenty-four hour period. If you do, you will cloud your reading and will not only get an inaccurate answer but will also waste your time and energy and that of your guides and angels. You will also give the impression that you are not listening and merely playing games with your fortune. Remember that you are able to receive a good reading to know your future without repeating the question too many times.

Pick up your cards, concentrate on your question, and cut the cards into three stacks, face down, placing the cards from left to right into three stacks facing you. If you are reading for a person across the table from you, you still read the cards from left to right.

Turn the cards over using this method of a yes or no question. Look at the three stacks.

Three red mean yes.

Two red mean maybe.

One red means no.

Alternatively,

Three black mean no.

Two black, probably not.

One black, yes.

PLAYING CARDS
THE THREE CARD READING

The second method of reading the playing cards is to ask the question, What is most important in your future?

Take your playing cards and lay them all out face down into a fan-shape in front of you.

Using your dominate hand, choose three cards, laying each of the three cards face up in front of you, from left to right. Just as with the dice and the dominoes, the position of the cards should lay in order of left to right, position one, two, and three, respectively.

Position one is the card furthest to your left, position two is the middle card, and position three is the card furthest to your right.

1. The far left position, position one, signifies the subject.

2. The middle position, position two, signifies how the subject relates to you.

3. The far right position, position three, signifies the outcome.

Put all three cards together to create a sentence, taking into consideration both the meaning of the card and the meaning of the position of the card. At the end of this chapter is a complete listing of the meaning of each of the cards. Use these meanings to give yourself a fortune telling reading from the playing cards. Again, remember that the meaning of each of the cards could be taken either literally or figuratively.

For example, choose three cards and read them together. Their description will give you a fortune. Let's say you pick the nine of hearts, the king of diamonds and a two of spades.

First look at the nine of hearts in the first position. This is your wish card and is considered a very positive card. This card is yes to the wish of which you are asking. So know that your fortune is going to be positive. Love is coming your way.

The king of diamonds signifies a male who is very social and who is out for himself. Because the nine of hearts lays adjacent to the king of diamonds in the second position, this tells you that this person who is going to be in your future has a love for you and his characteristic of getting what he wants will be in your favor.

Looking at the last card, the two of spades in the third position of outcome; this card signifies a bad union between two people.

Sadly to say, this relationship will start out great but according to your fortune cards, the person who is represented as the king of diamonds will be a disappointment for you and will turn against you in the end.

You can practice this type of reading as many times as you wish, but know that after five or six times of repeating this type of reading for the same question, your accuracy will become diluted.

PLAYING CARDS
THE LUCKY U-SHAPED READING

The third way of telling your fortune with the playing cards is to lay all of your playing cards face down into a fan-shape in front of you. Using your dominate hand, pull out nine playing cards.

You may only perform this type of card reading once in a twenty-four hour period. Accordingly, ensure that you have taken the time to properly infuse your cards with your energy during the shuffle before pulling the nine cards for the Lucky U-Shaped Reading.

When you pull the nine cards from the fan, you will lay the cards face up into a u-shape, three cards vertically down to your left, three cards across the middle horizontally from left to right, and three cards vertically up to your right.

> The three cards to your left represent the past.
>
> The three cards in the middle represent the present.
>
> The three cards to the right represent the future.

Interpret the three cards just as you did with the three card spread, reading the first three cards on the left as your past, the three cards in the middle as your present, and the three cards to the right as your future.

Take your time and consider the many different ways of deciphering the cards' descriptions. Remember, some cards have more than one meaning, and some meanings are literal and some meanings are figurative. This is an excellent exercise for your sixth sense.

Let's say you have drawn all hearts and diamonds in your u-shaped reading, for example, but you sense that something is still not right. For the next question you might ask, What is not right, then pull one card from the fan. Look at this card closely. If it is a face card then it is simple because the cards have shown you the face of the person who is causing the stress and uneasiness in your future.

But sometimes you will need to become more of a detective to discover the source of your feelings of uneasiness. For example, many years ago when I was reading the cards I continued to feel stress despite having drawn good cards. I subsequently pulled four different cards, all numbers. Oddly, the numbers seemed familiar to me. It was not until later, however, when I discovered that my friend had sabotaged my career situation and had taken my position, that I realized those four numbers were the last four digits of my friend's phone number.

I thank my guides and angels for not allowing me to see the future, only to be warned, because later as the cards had also shown, I was offered a better position at another business. I was grateful, because had I known that my friend at the time was collaborating to get my job, I would have reacted differently and could have changed fate. This is just another example of our sixth sense ensuring that we are on our path.

HEARTS

Hearts represent light-haired people, water signs and situations of a romantic nature.

Ace of Hearts

The ace of hearts represents a visit and your home environment. This is the love card, and when this shows up in a reading you will have a very positive loving relationship in your house.

King of Hearts

The king of hearts represents someone who has the ability to do something good for you. An older man with a very good nature who has an interest in your well being.

Queen of Hearts

The queen of hearts represents a fair-haired older woman who has a great deal of knowledge who can be trusted. She is very faithful to you and will always play fairly in what life deals her.

Jack of Hearts

The jack of hearts is a young man or young woman who is a very good friend to you. This could be a cousin or a close relative, someone you have known since your childhood.

Ten of Hearts

The ten of hearts is a good card, and it means good luck. This card can counteract negative cards that are around it.

Nine of Hearts

The nine of hearts card represents harmony and is often called the wish card. This is a great card to get. Even if you have negative cards surrounding it, this card showing itself in your reading will let you know that you will overcome the negative cards, that they are only obstacles, and that your wish will come true for your future.

Eight of Hearts

The eight of hearts is the party event card saying that some sort of celebration is taking place. You will be going to a party very soon.

Seven of Hearts

The seven of hearts is a card of disappointment. This card usually indicates someone not keeping their promises to you or that the plans that they have made with you will fall through.

Six of Hearts

The six of hearts is a warning card. Someone may be trying to take advantage of you. You may be being too generous to someone, and you are not going to get anything back in return.

Five of Hearts

The five of hearts is the power of relationship and love. The decision about love will be favorable if you have positive cards around it and negative if you have negative cards around it.

Four of Hearts

The four of hearts is the bachelor or old maiden card. It represents someone who will most likely end up living-out their life alone due to their own decision. It also can mean that you are being too hard on someone and should be grateful for their help. Be careful that you are not nitpicking anyone when you receive this card.

Three of Hearts

The three of hearts signifies a decision that was made without doing all of your background work first. Not a wise decision and made too quickly. You will regret this decision.

Two of Hearts

The two of hearts is the card of success. Most of the time, better than you had even thought. If you have other negative cards around it, there will simply be a delay in receiving that which you want. This is a very good card to receive.

CLUBS

Clubs represent brown-to-dark-haired individuals, earth signs and physical objects. Money, business and financial subjects.

Ace of Clubs

The ace of clubs is a very good card for wealth and fame. This card in your fortune means that new and old friends and acquaintances are drawn to you. You will be well known because of your physical looks and social status. You are a success.

King of Clubs

The king of clubs represents a very good, positive businessman. A male who is able to be trusted and counted upon. A shoulder to cry on and a friend who will help you when you are financially down.

Queen of Clubs

The queen of clubs is a woman who is not only very good at business, but also someone with a great deal of knowledge and power. She will help you like a partner. If this card is being interpreted as a male, this male has a very feminine side but is very good with finance.

Jack of Clubs

The jack of clubs represents someone who is very close with you, someone who likes to utilize compliments and verbal praise to cheer you up. This is someone who will also go-to-bat for you when you are not able to attend meetings.

Ten of Clubs

The ten of clubs is a great card of happiness and good fortune. It brings with it a very good, positive business trip that can be productive for you on your road to success.

Nine of Clubs

The nine of clubs is trouble and suggests that you will lose a relationship and may have some quarrels with relationships around you. Problems need to be resolved before you can move past this card.

Eight of Clubs

The eight of clubs - financial desire is what this card represents. What the other cards around it suggest will be your outcome of whether you are able to financially handle the situation or are not able to handle the situation. This can also be a card of bankruptcy.

Seven of Clubs

The seven of clubs is a card of very good fortune and if other positive cards are around this card, you can be assured of your success. Be careful of the individuals with whom you are having financial dealings who do not have your interests at heart. Do not mix business with pleasure at this point.

Six of Clubs

The six of clubs is the partnership card. Success based upon mutual goals and friendship. This is a good financial partnership for you at this time. If all of the other cards around this card are positive, this will be a successful financial card for your family.

Five of Clubs

The five of clubs is the marriage card. This is also a good card for beginning a business partnership with long term goals because this card suggests that your future will do well working with others to make you successful.

Four of Clubs

The four of clubs is a misfortune card. This is not a very good card regarding allies in that when this card shows up in your fortune, others can go against you at the drop of a hat. Best to go-it-alone when you see this card.

Three of Clubs

The three of clubs is a change of relationship card. This card is usually a sign of a second or third marriage or commitment. You should look at the cards around this card to see your outcome.

Two of Clubs

The two of clubs is a very bad luck card. You will be let down by those people around you and will not have any support from friends or family. This is not a time to count on anyone. Usually this card suggests that you will need to change your path course to find true happiness.

DIAMONDS

Diamonds represent darker-blond-to-reddish-haired people, the element of air (this is "old school"), and they represent social people and events and gatherings in your life.

Ace of Diamonds

An ace of diamonds means there is a message coming into your life that will be very positive and socially beneficial for you. Pay attention to what others like right now. You should trend with what is in style.

King of Diamonds

The king of diamonds is a man who is very much a social climber and who will stop at nothing to reach his goals. If you know of someone who is your friend and this card is in your future reading, know that this person may be helping you to help himself. If you do not know of anyone or you are a female, be careful now that someone does not try to be deceitful toward you to get what they want.

Queen of Diamonds

The queen of diamonds is a very attractive female who will use all of her social graces to get what she wants. If you are much of a politically-geared person you will want to make friends with her because she can connect you with the right people. If you do not like politics, stay clear of her. This card states that a woman in your life who enjoys the ball more than the people at the party could be your downfall.

Jack of Diamonds

The jack of diamonds represents someone who you cannot trust what they say and who likes to speak of subjects that are not to be spoken of. Things that others wish would have remained unsaid. Remember when you get this card to not always believe everything you hear but only what you see. Your true friends will stand by you during this time.

Ten of Diamonds

The ten of diamonds suggests financial means coming into your life to which you might want to first confirm that there are no strings attached. By using these finances, you could be in a great deal of trouble and the money will sift through your fingers. Just be careful with your finances if you have received this card.

Nine of Diamonds

A nine of diamonds in your reading suggests you will have a great event or sequence of events that will lead to a very good time in your life. Sit back and ride the tide of life, but remember to smell the roses along the way. A very good card.

Eight of Diamonds

The eight of diamonds is a card that is telling you to definitely slow down and smell the roses. You are in a social and physical dilemma that needs to completely not only slow down but you need to change the way you are doing things before you end up in an overly-stressed and unhealthy condition.

Seven of Diamonds

The seven of diamonds is the card that conveys you should avoid dealings involving any new ideas at this time. Keep your own counsel, keep to yourself, and do not ask others. Look inside. Doing anything that is somewhat of a gamble should be avoided right now. Someone is testing you to see if they can pull the wool over your eyes.

Six of Diamonds

The six of diamonds card in your fortune suggests that the person you love now is not the person you will be with later. This is not a time to be swept off your feet. Try to keep a clear head because you do not know everything about the person who is trying to woo you for attention.

Five of Diamonds

The five of diamonds is a very good card with your family and children. You will have much to be grateful for. Be careful that you do not brag so much about your own blessings but are able to help those who are not so blessed.

Four of Diamonds

The four of diamonds indicates there will likely be problems in your house and home. Some of the family will want to celebrate while others feel that you are a stick-in-the-mud. Make sure to participate in a family outing.

Three of Diamonds.

The three of diamonds is the card of problems at home. Be careful of upsetting or agitating a situation that has reached the point of seeking out legal aid.

Two of Diamonds

The two of diamonds represents someone who loves because they want to draw attention to themselves. If you are a married person, this is a warning that someone has a crush on you and this person is not concerned if they hurt you or a loved one. If you are single and want to begin a social stir, you are about to get what you want. Someone is ready to give the people around you something to talk about.

SPADES

Spades are dark-haired people, the element of fire, and represent warnings and unforeseen events that are not always pleasant.

Ace of Spades

The ace of spades is very bad news. Loss of something or someone near you. This card can last for years and you should take heed when you have this card in your reading. Many situations are not in your favor at this time.

King of Spades

The king of spades is a man who causes problems in relationships or marriage or possibly even your marriage. He is able to destroy whatever relationships you have if he does not feel that it is to his benefit. Be careful of a dark-haired older man in your life at this time. Usually if you receive this card, you will know exactly who he is and what he is up to. If not, know that if you have had a problem with him, he is devising your destruction as you read this. Take heed. This is a very strong card.

Queen of Spades

The queen of spades is a betrayal by a woman who will go to any and all means to get what she wants. She has a very sharp tongue and cares not who she hurts and also, like the king of spades, will stop at nothing to get what she wants in life. Let's just hope that you are not in the way of her life's plans or she will take you out of the situation using all means at her disposal.

Jack of Spades

This is not a bad person, the jack of spades, this is a lazy person who will get whatever he can get out of you without having to give very much back in return. Know that you are not worth the effort to him, so this is not a very solid friendship.

Ten of Spades

The ten of spades is a very unlucky card. If near a good card, it can cancel-out the good card. If there are many other negative cards around this card, this card will make it twice as bad.

Nine of Spades

The nine of spades is the worst card of all. This card is letting you know of illness, loss of money, misery and even among the best of cards, you will be defeated in receiving your success. Success is very unlikely. It is highly unlikely that you will have anything good come from your actions at this time in your life.

If this card has shown in your reading, this is a time to step back from life and make some serious decisions on how you can create success elsewhere than where you are presently, because life is about to give you a very sharp turn in your path.

Eight of Spades

The eight of spades is telling you that these are people who are not your friends. You cannot trust the people with whom you are social with at this time. Be sure that you have all of your ducks in a row before doing anything with the crowd that you are hanging with or you may find yourself up a creek without a paddle.

Seven of Spades

The seven of spades is a very bad card for friendships, and you should let other people believe what they want to believe. Do not get into arguments or discussions of a serious nature right now. Just let everything ride. Everything will be better after this has passed.

Six of Spades

The six of spades is the card of little results. Hard work without much profit. You can expect disappointment even though you have always been able to work your way out of a situation. This is a time that is very discouraging.

Five of Spades

The five of spades represents success in business and love after much time and hard work. One of the few spades cards that represents a positive outcome. By working very hard and diligently, you will have love and success.

Four of Spades

The four of spades is the set-back card. Possibly feeling not well for awhile and you will be set back with your goals for awhile. It may not last forever but will keep you delayed for a short time.

Three of Spades

The three of spades is the card of unhappiness. It is the card of disappointment. Do not let this action hold you back. It is best to trudge onward to a brighter future.

Two of Spades

The two of spades signifies a dramatic change in your life. You will be changing some major events in your life such as job, location, and possibly relationship or even unfortunately there may be a sudden death.

Guide to Reading the Palm as a Tool

THERE ARE SO MANY EXCELLENT PALMISTRY readings and different ways to interpret the lines and types of hand shapes, that for the purpose of this guide book where we are utilizing this ability as a tool to heighten one's sixth sense, the exercise is kept very simple and very easy to understand.

First, lay your hand which is not dominant on the table, opened. Ask the subject you are reading to lay their dominant hand on top of your hand so that you may read their hand. Ask permission, as with any of these tools, so that they and their spiritual guides and angels know your intention. To give respect and spiritual privacy, always ask another person permission to read them.

After the person has given consent, take your dominant hand over their hand which they have laid on yours, and place your index and middle finger on the mound right under their thumb on the fleshy part of the hand. Relaxing and rubbing lightly on this mound, you will feel the Mars mound. This mound conveys the individual's headstrongness, ego, and personality. Just by relaxing and feeling this mound, you can tell if this person is headstrong, wishy-washy, a decision maker or a follower. You will know this by sensing the feeling of this mound.

A strong decision maker will have a very high, rounded mound at the base of the thumb, whereas a person who is indecisive and wishy-washy will have an indented feeling there. You will be surprised at how immediately you can sense and feel this with the person.

Continue around the hand to the index finger on the hand. Just before the finger, right at the base of the index finger, is the Jupiter mound. This mound controls business and career and also luck. If the mound is very strong and very firm, you have a very lucky person who has a financially solid life. Once again, if the mound is indented or shallow, this person has fallen upon unfortunate circumstances in the career, perhaps changing jobs frequently.

You should now move your hand back toward the Mars mound, sensing what you felt the first time there, putting both sensations together. If the person appears as a headstrong person but upon going back to the Jupiter mound displays deep indentations and has lived a hard life, you will sense this and feel this. Simply add what else you begin to feel within your energy. Oftentimes you will perceive other sensations of the person through these mounds. Say what you feel; go with your first impression and never go against your gut feeling. This will be what your sixth sense is telling you about that individual.

The next mound is under the middle finger of the person's hand. You will notice the mound beneath the middle finger can be very hardened or very soft. This is the Saturn mound and the mound of karma. Notice that you will perceive a very hardened karma around a person who is an older soul who has experienced a great deal of spiritual lessons in this life, where a softened mound is a very young soul who is still learning their spiritual path.

The next finger, the ring finger, is the Venus mound. This is the love and relationship mound of the person you are reading. Oftentimes you will feel lines on this mound or even actual bumps. No bumps, no lines, the person has never known true love. The feeling that you have from this mound is usually an emotional feeling. Obviously, a positive emotional feeling means this person has found someone and a sad, negative feeling from this mound means this person has never been with someone in love or is experiencing challenges in the relationship.

Last but not least, at the base of the little pinky finger of your subject's hand is the Mercury mound. This is the mound of socializing, communication, indicating other individuals in this person's life such as children, family and coworkers. As you touch this mound, notice the temperature of this mound. If this mound is warm or vibrant, this person is sociable and good with people. A mound that feels a little cool to your fingertip and maybe a little shallow is someone who is antisocial and not a very caring, loving person at this time.

Remember, most of this exercise is done with your physical sensation of touching the person's mounds, and you should always remember that the hand does change every twenty-eight days. The actual fingerprints of a person's hand do not change, but the actual mounds and indentations do change. A good example is that of a client I have read four times. Twice of those four times, on her palm a very strong, star-shaped symbol was displayed. This star-shaped symbol is a symbol of fame and fortune. Both times that this star was displayed in her hand were times when she was associated with someone who has a very well-known name. Her energy and aura field were associating her with this fame. After she and the person had successfully completed their work together and had separated, the aura field and energy of the person with fame also had vanished. The star symbol on this client's hand had vanished with no trace to be found.

Remember to have fun with this exercise. Read the mounds and the energies of people who you have never met along with people who you know. You will be surprised at how quickly you are able to read more than just these mounds. The mounds are a great tool to awaken your sixth sense and to provide an easy way to sense another individual's future.

10
Spiritual Cleansing

ANY TIME THAT YOU ARE ACTIVELY involved with spiritual activities such as raising your energy vibration, clearing your chakras or developing your psychic abilities and intuition, you should periodically, at least once a month, perform a spiritual cleansing on yourself and on your surroundings. Such cleansings include saging your home, salt baths, and yes, sometimes sun baths. These practices should be a regular activity in your life. You will be able to use these exercises to help yourself and others in your spiritual development. For the purpose of cleansing your energies in order to develop your sixth sense, I will share with you an easy yet effective exercise of spiritual cleansing.

WHITE CARNATION CLEANSING

For this exercise you will need a bouquet of white carnations. You can find white carnations at any florist and oftentimes at the larger grocery markets. You will also need a brown paper bag such as a grocery bag or a smaller-sized brown paper bag such as a lunch bag or a liquor store bag; size does not matter but the material does. It must be a brown paper bag. You will need three brown paper bags for this exercise.

Plan to perform this exercise at the time of day where you are at your best. Let's say you are a morning riser and like the morning hours, which is where you feel most comfortable. Do this exercise between 8:00 a.m. and noon. If you are more of a person who awakens later in the day around 10:00 a.m. or noon and begin to enjoy the day at this time, you should do the exercise between noon and 4:00 p.m. If you are a person working the swing shift from the approximate 2:00 p.m. to 10:00 p.m. time slot, then you should do this exercise between 4:00 p.m. and 8:00 p.m. on a day where you are not working during these hours. Anyone who works the graveyard shift or who is nocturnal should do this exercise between 8:00 p.m. and midnight. Never do this exercise after midnight or before 8:00 a.m.

The cleansing exercise is very simple and consists of first separating the bouquet of carnations into three equal bunches. For example, if you have fifteen flowers in the bouquet, place five separate stems together to make three equal bunches. It is not so important that you have exactly nine blossoms divided into three and three and three as it is that you make the bunches of equal size. If you have an extra flower or two, place them in a vase somewhere in your home where you spend most of your time. This will help cleanse the energy in your home, as carnations absorb negative energy.

Once you have divided the flowers into three bunches, place one brown paper bag with each bunch of flowers: three bags, three bunches.

This exercise is most effective when it is performed within a time frame of four hours, so allow yourself time in your schedule to complete the entire four hours of the exercise.

First, take one bunch of flowers with you into the shower. Take a normal shower using the flowers, leaves, stems and all, as a washcloth. Stand with only warm water in the shower: no soap, no deodorant, only water, you and the flowers. Using the flowers, stems, leaves and all as a washcloth, recite The Lord's Prayer. As you pray, also concentrate on using the stems and the flowers to rinse and cleanse your energy so that none of the negative energies that are in our world today are able to stay within your aura field.

The carnations will absorb the energies and help cleanse your aura by taking this negative energy from your energy field. This also helps reduce stress, negative vibrations, and even clears psychic links in your aura field. Make sure that you are verbally and mentally reciting The Lord's Prayer while beginning at the top of your body and washing down all over your body, especially your feet. Hold on to the wall so that you may wash even the bottom of your feet where you stand.

After you have completed the first step, leave the carnations in the shower, and turn off the water. You will need to air-dry. Depending upon the climate where you live, allow yourself to air-dry for a minimum of ten minutes up to, in more humid areas, thirty minutes. Do not towel dry, which entails rubbing or patting a towel against your body to dry because you will be rubbing the energy back into your aura. Let the air and the carnations remove it from your energy field.

After you have allowed ten to thirty minutes of air-drying time, you can now dress yourself. Next, using the opposite hand of the hand you write with, not your dominant hand, pick up the flowers from the shower and place them into the brown paper bag you have set aside for them. You must close the brown paper bag and tighten the top of the bag, closing the top of the bag. Carry the brown paper bag enclosing the carnations and remove the bag and carnations from your physical property. Carry them into a dumpster off of your property, such as a dumpster or trash can at a convenience store. Do not place them in a trash can within your home.

Repeat the process with the second bunch of flowers just as you have with the first. Wash with carnations, recite The Lord's Prayer, leave the carnations in the shower, air-dry, remove the carnations from the property, and repeat this process for the third time.

After you have done this with all three bunches of flowers, you have now cleansed your aura. Sometimes you may begin to feel groggy or tired. This is a perfect time to finish with the one hour that remains of your time. For this final basic meditation exercise, lie down in a calm, safe, secure place in your home. Visualize breathing-in light, positive energy, visualizing the very positive light around a full, mid-day sun. As you inhale, visualize breathing-in the light through your nose and filling your lower, red chakra with this light energy. Raise the chakra's energy as you go through each of your seven chakras, just relaxing and feeling your body fill with light, positive energy. You will feel this energy very much strengthening your chakras as the light begins to balance out the energy, revitalizing each and every part of your body. Begin with your feet, moving up through your legs, moving up through your hips and torso and eventually up through your head. As you inhale, visualize breathing-in the light and as you exhale, visualize breathing out everything that is cold or unpleasant from your body.

This simple exercise amounts to about four hours and has a very profound effect on the physical aura. For those able to see energy, the energetic change can be described as transformational. I have witnessed significant changes in clients' auras for over thirty years.

Clients may suffer an unclean aura because of negative energy perhaps from being surrounded throughout the day by negative people or employees at their work place. They experience headaches, nausea, low energy, and uncertainty in their lives. After one of these cleansings they will be revitalized, oftentimes realizing that the person who has been sending them the negative intent is someone at work. Until this point, they had simply been tolerating the negativity, not realizing the impact of the person's negative intent upon their physical aura.

A healthy aura should look like a smooth, egg-shaped energy field around the physical body. Again, each person has his own color of aura depending upon moods, intellect, spirituality and beliefs. Oftentimes a person who is experiencing problems will have a clouded aura and negative blotches of energies on their aura. These negative energies cause interference between a person's spiritual guides and angels and the person's gut feelings and spiritual information. This interference will cause an individual oftentimes distress and confusion, or at minimum, lack of clarity.

After the cleansing above, an individual can accurately determine the true color of their aura. For example, a person who is very spiritual and able to communicate well, often has an aura that is blue. But if the person is experiencing negative energies, the aura would appear more of a greenish and odd, yellow color. The negative influences around the aura cause interference with the high frequency of the aura. The negative energy is cleansed from the body: the carnations having removed the negativity from the person, the person by taking the carnations to the convenience store or dumpster off of the property thereby demonstrating the intent of removing the negative energies from their life, thus leaving only their chakras to work and move at the vortex position to raise the energy to the blue level which is a higher frequency.

Oftentimes you will physically see something on the carnations. Even if you cannot, those with their third eye open such as myself have seen negative energies such as what I consider to look like spit from a grasshopper or tobacco juice. This is what I witness going down the drain and all over the carnations after the completion of even one of the many various types of spiritual cleansings. Significantly, the number three is a spiritual vibration, and performing this three times is using the number of the trinity.

The reasoning for the paper bag is that the paper originates from wood. The tree also helps absorb energy and places a natural boundary around the carnations and the negative energy. Plastic does not do this. You are being protected from what is on the flowers by the brown paper bag because the paper originates from trees and because trees are able to absorb the negativity. Again, plastic does not have this quality of the element and will not prohibit the negativity from being drawn back to you.

This spiritual cleansing was handed-down to me from my third metaphysical teacher. It was handed-down to my third metaphysical teacher from his mother, a well-known spiritual healer. I suggest performing this spiritual cleansing once every couple of months.

FROM THE AUTHOR

The purpose of this book has been to help each and every person who has ever experienced a sensation from the sixth sense such as knowing who is on the phone before picking it up; the feeling that someone you know is thinking about you right before the person shows up at your house; predicting what is wrong with a person's health even though you have just met the person for the first time and know nothing of their medical records; knowing immediately a person's future and events that will take place by simply having touched their hand; or having a mental flash of events that are coming up later in this person's life.

This guide book provides some basic tools using household items that will not only strengthen the ability to read your own and another individual's energy but will also enable you to enjoy heightening your sixth sense by performing the simple exercises.

All of the tools such as the dice, the dominoes, and the playing cards are only objects that are being utilized by you and your own personal energy. The items will be objects to use at any time on which to focus your energies so that you are able to develop and utilize your abilities. Enjoy!

ABOUT THE AUTHOR

JETHRO SMITH, PART NATIVE AMERICAN INDIAN, is a natural-born intuitive whose gift heightened after a near-death experience. In kindergarten he began reading his friends' auras, communicating with loved ones who had crossed over, and foreseeing future events.

Extraordinarily gifted from birth, Jethro was intensely tested and mentored by Master Teachers beginning preschool throughout his twenties, enabling him to control and to develop his abilities in a positive manner. Jethro has been professionally helping others for over 30 years.

Jethro believes that everyone is born with the intuitive gift and has the ability to use this insight to grow spiritually.

Jethro is certified and registered in *The United States National Register of Tested, Certified and Bona Fide Lightworkers, Psychics and Mediums* and *The World's Best and Most Trusted Psychics, Mediums and Healers* and is listed in *Covington Who's Who*. He is a Certified Reiki Master and is founder and host of the award winning blog talk radio show Psychics Gone Wild. He is the author of Living in the Psychic Realm.

www.ingramcontent.com/pod-product-compliance
Lightning Source LLC
LaVergne TN
LVHW040155080526
838202LV00042B/3172